The Patriot King; Or Irish Chief: A Tragedy

Francis Dobbs

THE
PATRIOT KING;

OR

IRISH CHIEF.

A

TRAGEDY.

Performed at the THEATRE in SMOCK-
ALLEY, DUBLIN.

By FRANCIS DOBBS.

===

LONDON:

Printed for J. BEW, No. 28, *Paternoster-Row*, and
A. GRANT, No. 5, *Bridges-street, Covent-Garden.*
M.DCC.LXXIV.

To the Right Honourable

The COUNTESS of ELY.

MADAM,

ENCOURAGED by the readinefs with which you patronifed the IRISH CHIEF, when reprefented on the *Dublin* Stage, I have ventured to offer that performance to the world, under the fanction of your Ladyfhip's name. I hope you will pardon the liberty I have taken in doing fo, without firft obtaining your permiffion. I fhould not have prefumed fo far, had not your Ladyfhip been pleafed to exprefs your approbation of my play, when I had the honour of laying it before you at *Rathfarnham*.

I am

I am convinced it would be highly difagreeable to you, were I to purfue the common mode of Dedications: I fhall therefore refrain from a fubject, on which I could with pleafure expatiate; and fhall only beg leave to affure you, that I am, with the greateft refpect,

Your Ladyfhip's Moft devoted

And moft grateful humble Servant,

FRANCIS DOBBS.

ADVER-

ADVERTISEMENT.

IT may not be unneceffary to acquaint the Reader, that this piece was performed in Dublin, at Smock-Alley Theatre, in April 1773.

The Author thought, from his obfervations during the performance, that many ufeful alterations, omiffions, and additions might be made; and he flatters himfelf that he has much improved his play fince that period.

The character of Cleones is entirely new, and of courfe the fcenes between him and Pharon (formerly Tor;) whofe paffion for Stira is alfo an addition.

The cataftrophe of this Tragedy was formerly unhappy, as Stira was really poifoned: the Author, however, hath yielded to the opinion of his friends, and has given a more fortunate conclufion.

The ingenious Mr. Melmoth, who filled the character of Ccallachan, made many judicious alterations in that part; but, as the Author cannot think of offering any thing in print to the public that is not

moft

moſt ſtrictly his own, he has entirely omitted them; and chooſes rather to want the ornaments of Mr. Melmoth's pen, than ſhine with borrowed luſtre.

The Author once had the higheſt ambition of being the compoſer of a well-received Tragedy: led away by youth and inexperience, he vainly hoped to ſucceed in his wiſhes, and, at the age of twenty-one, he firſt wrote the IRISH CHIEF. Time, however, hath ſince ſhown him his error, and he hath for ever relinquiſhed the idle expectation of Poetic Fame.

The Author of this piece will not be ſo illiberal as to rail at the Managers: his play has, without doubt, a thouſand imperfections, and perhaps a much greater number than are ſufficient to juſtify its rejection from the Theatres of Covent-Garden and Drury-lane: the Public, however, have ſometimes differed from the opinion even of a Mr. Garrick or a Mr. Coleman; and it is not impoſſible but they may allow as much merit to the IRISH CHIEF, as to a *Chriſtmas Tale*, an *Iriſh Widow*, or, a *Man of Buſineſs*.

PRO-

PROLOGUE.

Written by the AUTHOR:

To be spoken in the Character of CEALLACHAN.

H EAR me, ye Beaus : ye Critics, hear me too :
    By me, the Author humbly fues to you :
Requests your favour in his pending caufe ;
And from your kindnefs only, hopes applaufe.
That managers have furer means, we know—
Our Bard, alas ! no orders can beftow.

    'Midft many dangers, many dreadful fears,
One gleam of hope the affrighted Poet chears.
It muft be granted that his piece is new ;
And novelty, 'tis faid, you all purfue.

    Full oft hath honeft Teague been here difplay'd ;
And many a roar have Irifh blunders made :
The bull, the brogue, are now fo common grown ;
That one would almoft fwear they were—your own.
But, lo ! to-night, what you ne'er faw before,
A tragic hero from Hibernia's fhore ;
Who fpeaks as you do, both of men and things ;
And talks heroics, juft like other kings.

    Irifh heroics ! yonder Cit exclaims !
Who's been to Hackney, and has crofs'd the Thames :
Who forms his judgment from a few dull plays ;
And thinks a Porter's, is a nation's phrafe.

    To hold forth Nature, once the Stage was meant :
'Tis ftrangely alter'd from its firft intent.
Were we by it to judge Ierne's fons,
They all are honeft—but they all are clowns.
Yet truth hath faid, and I fhall take her word,
That fome have grac'd a court—and fome a cord.

    Know ye what part I act, who fpeak fo well ?
I'd lay my life not one in ten can tell :
So many lines without an Irifh howl,
Without by Jafus, or upon my fhoul :
'Tis ftrange indeed—nor can I hope belief,
When I declare myfelf, the IRISH CHIEF.

B

DRAMATIS PERSONÆ.

CEALLACHAN, King of Munfter, in love with STIRA,   Mr. MELMOTH.

DUNCAN, Friend to Ceallachan,   Mr. WILMOT.

SITRICK, Chief of the Danes in Ireland, and a Prince of the royal blood of Denmark,   Mr. SPARKS, jun.

PHARON, General to Sitrick, in love with Stira alfo,   Mr. KANE.

CLEONES, Friend to Pharon,   ————

BEDA, Wife to Sitrick, fecretly in love with Ceallachan,   Mrs. T. BARRY.

STIRA, Sifter to Sitrick, and in love with Ceallachan alfo,   Mrs. SPARKS.

OFFICERS, GUARDS, ATTENDANTS, &c.

SCENE, *DUBLIN*, and the Country adjacent.

THE

PATRIOT KING, &c.

ACT I.

SCENE, *Palace of* Dublin.

STIRA, BEDA.

STIRA.

AT length, my Beda, is the time arriv'd,
When anxious doubts and fears ſhall be no more.
The great Ceallachan this morning comes,
Comes to beſtow felicity ſupreme.
Not even Hope, with all her flatt'ring train,
Had promis'd to my wiſhes ſuch ſucceſs.

BEDA.

His virtues well I know, and own indeed,
His worth unrivall'd ſends its luſtre forth :
Yet ſtill 'tis ſtrange that Sitrick ſhould unite,

To Denmark's royal line, its greateſt foe.
What will each ſubjeƈt ſay, when they behold
Him who hath ſpilt their deareſt kindred's blood,
Thus honour'd by our chief---and thus eſpous'd?---

STIRA.

The Danes to virtue are not yet ſo loſt,
But they will give that praiſe his aƈtions claim ;
Nor can they blame the conduƈt that deſtroy'd---
No wanton quarrel urg'd him to the war:
To ſave his country from the Daniſh yoke
He drew his ſword ; and by his conqu'ring arm,
At once ſecur'd its freedom, and his crown.
Sitrick ſhould rather have his people's thanks
For making thus a deadly foe their friend,
Who ſtill hath brought diſhonour on their arms,
And ſent them vanquiſh'd from the field of death.

BEDA.

E'en ſhould the Danes theſe look'd-for rites approve,
Hath e'er this hero giv'n one proof of love ?
Seldom do princes from affeƈtion wed ;
To politics they oft muſt yield their choice.
Perhaps his people, tir'd of blood and war,
Requeſt him to accept thy offer'd hand,
And thus reſtore them to the ſweets of peace---
What then can Stira hope but cold reſpeƈt ?---
Will cold reſpeƈt repay a flame like thine ?

STIRA.

O Beda ! do not thus diſturb my mind,
Nor raiſe up thoughts that would for ever blaſt
My promis'd harveſt of unequall'd bliſs --
Did I not think his heart beat high with love,

Did

Did I not think that heart was wholly mine,
This hand fhould fooner end my hated life,
Than at the altar join Ceallachan's.---

BEDA.

Why then thefe hafty nuptials thus approve,
Whilft e'en fufpicion can afford a doubt?---

STIRA.

Why fhould I doubt? Do I not know he loves?
His eyes, thofe true revealers of the foul,
Have oft-times told me what his tongue with-held;
Each little act was with attention drefs'd,
And ev'ry look his tendernefs proclaim'd...
This is the language of a lover's heart,
This is the language that can ne'er deceive---

BEDA.

The mind that kindly feels for others woes,
With looks of foftnefs pours its ready balm,
And fteals affliction from the eye of forrow:
When firft ye met, you were a captive maid;
Impute not falfely to the pow'r of love,
What gen'rous pity might as well produce.

STIRA.

Oh, no! tho' pity in a heart like his,
Muft fympathife with ev'ry wretch's woe;
That foft regard which cannot be exprefs'd,
Nor yet mifunderftood, muft wanting be;
To mutual paffion it is only known,
And none but thofe who feel its pow'r believe.

Enter

Enter an Attendant to STIRA.

ATTENDANT.

Madam, a chief arriv'd from Munster's king
Requests admittance.

STIRA.

    Go bid him enter. [*Exit Attend.*
O my lov'd friend, a thousand fears arise---
But, lo! the valiant Duncan hither comes ?
Than him, none nearer to his monarchs thoughts---

Enter DUNCAN.

Most welcome, Sir---

BEDA.

    Most welcome to these walls---
How fares the king? Doth he still his purpose hold?
Hath ought prevented his intended speed?

DUNCAN.

Madam, the king with fondest ardour burns,
To meet his destin'd bride---one hour from hence,
He with impatience waits for my return.
Mean time, some secret thoughts for her I bear,
Whom soon I hope to call my queen.---

STIRA.

      Speak out.
Whate'er it is, 'tis safe in Beda's breast.---

DUNCAN.

This morn retir'd beneath a shady bow'r,
My royal Lord in terms like these, address'd
Mine ear---Go tell the lovely fair, he said,

        Whose

Whose charms unrivall'd rule thy monarch's heart,
That she alone can happiness beftow ;
Can give that blifs, which crowns might feek to buy,
Yet find the purchafe far beyond their reach.
But, oh ! my Duncan, tell the beauteous maid,
If in her breaft a dearer object lives,
Or fhould a brother's will her hand direct
Where inclination doth not prompt its courfe----
Oh ! tell her, I refign thefe promis'd rites,
And fingly wretched to my throne return.---

S T I R A.

Go tell the gen'rous prince from whom you came,
(For Stira's foul difdains her fex's arts)
That ev'ry future blifs on him depends---
Tell him, without a blufh I own my love,
And view with rapture the approaching hour,
That makes me ever his.---

D U N C A N.

                    ---Oh ! heavenly founds ;
Thus let me to my gracious princefs kneel,
And on her hand my faithful homage pay.----
Now to th' impatient king I'll quickly fly ;
And give a tranfport never felt before.   [Exit.

S T I R A.

Each doubting thought begone---with equal flame
His bofom glows, and Stira is moft blefs'd --
In pleafing tranfport ev'ry nerve is wrap'd---
My heart as if impatient to take flight,
And fpring to where its wifhes long have been,
Is fcarce contain'd in this, its little cell---
Beda forgive the raptures of a lover—

                                        Some

Some ordinary cares demand me now ;
This morning paſt, love claims each future hour.---

[*Exit.*

Manet BEDA.

To one unpractis'd in deceit, how hard
To wear a ſmile whilſt daggers pierce the heart,
And ſeem delighted with what wounds it moſt.
Theſe nuptials make a wretch of me indeed.---
Sure happineſs can ne'er that boſom fill,
Where paſſion prompts, what honor muſt forbid---
This king belov'd by me, by Sitrick's wife,
Now haſtes to wed the ſiſter of my lord---
Diſtraction!---what!---am I then doom'd to ſee
The man my heart adores, another's---No---
That, that, I cannot bear.---I'll to my huſband,
With Daniſh pride inflame his haughty ſoul,
And ſtop theſe rites, ſo fatal to my peace.   [*Exit.*

SCENE *changes to a different Part of*
Dublin.

Enter PHARON *and* CLEONES.

PHARON.

O my Cleones, I knew not till this hour,
The wondrous height my paſſion hath attain'd :
The beauteous Stira mingles with each wiſh,
Beats in each pulſe, and throbs thro' ev'ry vein :
---And ſhall this day beſtow her on another ?
Firſt ſhall this hand implant a dagger here,
Or ſheath one in the heart of Munſter's king.

CLEO.

CLEONES.

What madnefs doth poffefs thy heated mind?
This Stira never can be thine---even grant
Ceallachan thefe nuptials had refus'd ;
What hopes for thee remain'd?---Sitrick, thou know'ft,
Beholds even kings with fcorn ;---fo high he rates
The ancient honours of his royal line.

PHARON.

Where is the mighty merit to defcend
From kings, who trace their boafted anceftry
Even from the fabled Deities of Heav'n?
Flows there a richer current thro' the veins?
Pants in the breaft a more exalted worth?
Doth clay ennobled, purify the foul;
Or give a virtue humbler birth denies?---

CLEONES.

No, Pharon ; but the world is here the judge ;
We may condemn, not alter its decree.
Yet fay, had Fortune been a kinder dame,
How would the beauteous Stira be difpofed?
Doth fhe behold thee with a partial eye,
And blufh compliance on thy wifhes?

PHARON.

                    ---Alas!

No tender glance hath e'er allay'd my pain,
No fweet confufion blufh'd a kind confent ;
Yet do I love her to that pitch of frenzy,
She muft, fhe fhall be mine---

CLEONES.

                    ---She muft be yours!---
O impotence of paffion !---Doth not this hour,

C   This

This very hour, bestow her on another,
And blast thy foolish hopes for ever?---

PHARON.

                ---This hour,
If Fortune favours, gives her to my arms---
For know, my friend, e'en now the ready bark
Unfurls her canvass to the coming winds,
Spreads every sail to catch the precious breeze,
And waft us from Ierne's shore---

CLEONES.

                ---What then
Can Pharon stoop, thus meanly to possess
The injur'd form of weeping innocence?---
Think'st thou Love's holy raptures can be thine?
When, not the soft murmurs of the yielding maid,
Nor yet the sweet resistance beauty gives,
But tears and harsh complaints assail thine ear,
Pierce thro' thy heart, and load thee with remorse:
Then Pharon wilt thou curse this hateful day,
And damn that hour which gave thee being---

PHARON.

                ---O stop---
Recall not feelings that were lull'd to rest;
But lend thy aid to bear the fair one hence:
Let Pharon clasp this charmer to his breast,
And revel in ecstatic scenes of bliss.

CLEONES.

Such are indeed the scenes of mutual love---
When the fond female in each look declares
The rising tumults of a soft desire:
When, fearful of sensations yet unknown,

The blufhing maid with downcaft eye confents,
And trembling fills a lover's arms---then, then
Indeed, to clafp her to the panting breaft,
To foothe with all the eloquence of love,
And drive thofe idle fears away---is blifs,
Is ecftacy divine !---But you, my Lord,
Oh! what have you to hope ?---you---

PHARON.

     ---Cleones ceafe---
At once declare there's danger in the tafk
That Friendfhip hath requir'd ; nor meanly feek
To hide thy fears beneath the veil of honour.--

CLEONES.

You are unkind, my Lord ; I might fay more :
Where obligations bind the heart, the obliger
Should be more delicate---

PHARON.

     ---And the obliged
More grateful.---

CLEONES.

   ---More grateful cannot be---
Had you but bade me rufh on certain death,
You fhould have feen how little life was priz'd.
My honour is, I own, a dearer ftake ;
Nor can ev'n gratitude oblige Cleones
To part with virtue.---

PHARON.

   ---This wond'rous virtue too
No doubt will make thee hafte to Sitrick's prefence,
And all my fcheme betray.----

    C 2   CLEONES.

CLEONES.

      ---Fear not, my Lord:
You ſpoke in friendſhip, as a friend I heard.
So ſacred is ſuch converſe held by me,
That racks and tortures ſhould extort in vain.
The poſt, which, by your favour was obtain'd,
I here reſign---And now, my Lord, farewell---
You'll eaſy find a more obſequious friend;
A truer is perhaps beyond your reach.

                                       [Exit.

Manet PHARON.

  Oh! thou haſt touch'd me to the very ſoul,
Made me examine this my purpos'd deed,
And ſtruck a horror o'er the conſcious mind:
The very crime with which I raſhly charg'd thee
Rebounds upon myſelf---by Sitrick's power,
Plac'd in the firſt high office of the ſtate,
I ſeek to bear his lovely ſiſter hence,
And thus repay the bounteous hand that rais'd me.
Oh! I ſhall ſeek thee my Cleones,
Fall on thy neck, and wet thee with my tears,
Till thou, relenting, feel ſoft pity riſe,
And giv'ſt a pardon to repenting folly;
Then wilt thou teach me to regain repoſe,
And conquer paſſion, by the force of honour.

                                       [Exit.

Enter SITRICK, BEDA.

Scene changes to the Palace.

BEDA.

  Worthleſs would be the partner of thy bed,
If ſhe concealed ought affecting thee.

                                       The

The people murmur, and with loud outcry
Declare their hatred of thefe purpos'd rites.
Shall he, they fay, whofe fword fo oft hath reek'd
With fathers', brothers', and with kinfmens' gore,
Now light the nuptial torch amidft our grief!
Much more than this, they publicly declare:
Should Sitrick ftill perfift, Oh! who can tell
Where fuch repinings end!---

SITRICK.

---Thanks to thy love;
But Sitrick fears no danger from fuch threats.
E'er yet to-morrow bids the world adieu,
Their praife, not cenfure, fhall my zeal reward.

BEDA.

Truft not, my Lord, to fuch uncertain hopes,
Nor think to lead the mean, ignoble crowd,
By Reafon's force. In vain doth wifdom try
To calm their paffions, and their wrath reftrain:
When thoughtlefs fury fpurs, away they run,
And ev'ry ftep leaves judgment more behind.

SITRICK.

Fear not the prudent conduct of thy Lord;
Well fkill'd, I hold the reins of fov'reign pow'r,
Know when to treat men with an eafy hand,
And how to curb them in their mad career.

BEDA.

But grant thy people fhould their rage refign:
Can Sitrick ftoop to join his royal houfe
To Munfter's petty king?---Where now that pride,
Which once infpir'd the bofom of my lord?---
Haft thou forgiv'n that hand, fo oft uprear'd,

To

To pluck the laurel from thy brow, to blaſt
Thy glory, and o'erturn each conqueſt paſt,
By preſent ſhame and deep diſgrace.---

SITRICK.

---Forgiv'n !
But little doſt thou know the ſoul of Sitrick---
Vengeance alone, for wrongs like mine, atone.---

BEDA.

And as a proof of which, you ſeek to give
A ſiſter to his arms!---

SITRICK.

---Well may'ſt thou ſcorn
The ſeeming baſeneſs. Yet know, my Beda,
Such muſt the glorious ſequel be, that you,
Even you, ſhall give applauſe.---

BEDA.

---What ? ſhall I praiſe
The timorous dictates of a poor diſmay ?
Prudence perhaps may juſtify the deed ;
Perhaps the beauteous Sitra may perſuade
This conquering monarch to with-hold his arms,
And ſpare the timid Dane.---

SITRICK.

---Nay, taunt not thus---
The Danes no more ſhall feel his power---e'en now
Doth Munſter totter on the verge of ruin ;
And all her laurels fade, to bloom no more.---

BEDA.

Ha! what ſay'ſt thou ? explain thy doubtful words ?

SITRICK.

SITRICK.

The event my hidden meaning shall unfold.---

BEDA.

I pr'ythee, Sitrick, indulge my curious ear,
And let thy secret purpose be reveal'd.---

SITRICK.

Farewell---I know thy sex's weaknefs better---
Eager to hear, impatient to reveal;
Give but a fecret to the breaft of woman,
Some fav'rite female fhares the facred truft,
Who to another muft difclofe it too;
Till thus, 'tis whifper'd o'er a prying world.   [*Exit.*

Manet BEDA.

Thoughts rufh upon me, that increafe, not heal
The wounds within my breaft---Some dark defign,
Some deep-laid ftratagem my fears difplay,
Full of deftruction to th' Hibernian king;
Whofe open unfufpicious foul, ne'er thought
Of deeds in others which himfelf abhor'd.---
Sitrick is fubtle, cruel, and fo dead
To all the finer feelings of the mind,
Where honour dwells,---that virtue in a foe,
But heightens and inflames his rage.---Ah, why?
Allur'd by title and the farce of ftate,
Will woman throw her happinefs away?
I knew this Sitrick well, nay, loath'd him;
Yet caught by grandeur, gave my plighted faith;
Too late repentance wounds my tortur'd breaft,
Too late I feel an unavailing flame,
And prove the torment of a vain defire.   [*Exit.*

End of ACT FIRST.

ACT

ACT II.

SCENE, *Palace of* Dublin.

SITRICK, PHARON.

SITRICK.

DRAW near my faithful Pharon---ſtill haſt thou been
The partner of my counſels and my arms;
And ever have I found thee as I hop'd,
True to thy truſt, and loyal to thy prince.
Then know, that e'er this ſun revolves its courſe,
The man whom Sitrick calls his greateſt foe
Shall be no more---Ceallachan ſhall die.---

PHARON.

Shall die!---forgive the amazement that I feel
At ſuch a ſtrange reverſe, and let me aſk
What mean theſe gaudy preparations here,
That indicate the joyful bridal feaſt?
What meant the embaſſy to Munſter's court,
That offer'd gentle peace to all its realm,
And beauteous Stira to its monarch's bed?---

SITRICK.

Why, all was meant to make deſtruction ſure.
The wily ſerpent, e'er he ſtings, diſplays
A thouſand beauties to delight the eye,
And tempt the unwary traveller's approach;
Then quickly darts upon his certain prey:
Thus Munſter's king beholds fair Stira's charms,
Nor dreams that he advances to his fate.

PHARON.

PHARON.

But how accomplish this thy purpos'd scheme?
The world proclaims the wisdom of thy foe;
He sure requir'd some hostage of thy faith;
Nor trusts his person, without ample proof
Of safety to himself and to his train.

SITRICK.

Thou know'st him not, nor doth the foolish world;
It thinks him wise, I prove its judgment false---
No sooner did he spy the gilded bait,
Than down it went, quick as my wishes ask'd;
Nor shall he find the well disguised hook,
Till Sitrick, like a skilful angler, strike,
And undeceive him at the price of life.

PHARON.

But say, my lord, from whence thy plan arose;
And how conducted?---

SITRICK.

   ---Thou shalt hear, my friend.---
--When last---(perdition seize his conqu'ring arm)
When last Ceallachan o'ercame my troops,
And drove me vanquish'd from the bloody field;
My wife, my sister too, thou know'st were ta'en,
And led in triumph to the Irish court:
(But out of that shall spring my great revenge);
For there, the youthful monarch's amorous heart,
Open to love, receiv'd the piercing shaft,
And Stira's beauty all his soul subdu'd.---
Inform'd of this, I brought it to my aid,
And offer'd her the bond of future peace:
The lover fir'd with recollection strong

D   Of

Of all the graces of her lovely form,
Now haſtens here, nor once demanded ought
To bind the treaty, or ſecure himſelf.

PHARON.

Pardon, my Lord, the freedom of my tongue,
And hear thoſe cooler thoughts thy welfare prompts---
Tho' much I wiſh deſtruction on thy foe ;
Yet muſt I think, thy ſafety will forbid
To execute what now thou haſt propos'd :
Reflect on all thoſe valiant dauntleſs tribes
Ceallachan commands ;---whoſe meaneſt troops
Would gladly forfeit life for dear revenge :
Then image to thyſelf, reſentment rous'd
By ſuch a deed ; and prudence muſt declare
How fatal the attempt.---

SITRICK.

                       ---Prudence may paint
In ſtrongeſt lines each dreadful conſequence ;
But, by yon heav'n he dies: my mad'ning ſoul
Now rages with revenge, which nought can cool
But his deſtruction :---Let me but behold
His lifeleſs corſe, and all his hoſts may come.---

PHARON.

Since nought can change my prince's fix'd reſolve,
Let caution dictate what thy vengeance claims :
Let him be made the captive of thy arms :
Then may'ſt thou offer liberty and life,
On theſe conditions---that he'll ſtraight yield up
Each place of ſtrength and fortreſs in his ſway.---
If he conſents, his people's love is ſuch,
That they will ſure comply.---Then may we find

                                          Some

Some after-means to give the wifh'd-for death :
Thus fhall thy vengeance have its full demand,
And fafety be fecur'd.---

SITRICK.

                    ---Thou counfel'ft well ;
It fhall be fo.---But hafte, my Pharon, hafte;
Lead forth a chofen band, and quickly gain
The rear of Munfter's train---fhould ought infpire
Ceallachan with doubt, or in his mind
Sufpicion raife, this will prevent retreat.

                                        [*Exit.*

Manet PHARON.

    The profpect brightens, fhe may yet be mine,
Nor honour, nor Cleones interpofe---
Ha ! what will Cleones fay, when he beholds
The faith of nations, and of men betray'd---
When he beholds, perhaps, a monarch's blood
To vengeance fhed, and fpilt by Pharon's aid ?---
Oh, no ! that muft not be---I'll watch with care,
Each confcious fting that pierces Sitrick's breaft,
Difplay the horrors that await remorfe,
And change the bloody purpofe of his foul.

                                        [*Exit.*

SCENE *changes to a woody Country near* Dublin.

Enter *two* IRISH OFFICERS *in converfation.*

1ft OFFICER.

'Tis ftrange indeed---Duncan to Dublin gone,
The King in thought wrap'd up---All is not right---

        D 2   2d OFFICER.

2d OFFICER.

May Heav'n avert whate'er difturbs his peace:
Sure he whofe ample foul delights in all
That tends to aid the meaneft of mankind,
Can ne'er deferve a pang.---

1ft OFFICER.

    ---None are exempt
From life's mis-haps---But where's Ceallachan?
Haft lately feen him?

2d OFFICER.

    ---Yes,—e'en now we met;
He enter'd yonder wood, whofe leafy top
A pleafing umbrage fpreads, that foothes the mind
Where contemplation reigns, and leads it on
To pour its feelings forth beneath thofe bow'rs,
Whofe filent fhade our confidence invites---
Behold where now he walks, clofe to yon oak,
With folded arms;---with flow and thoughtful pace,
In awful meditation loft to all.

1ft OFFICER.

Let us retire, nor rudely interrupt
His folitary courfe---when thus inclin'd
For folitude and converfe with one's felf,
How irkfome even thofe whom moft we prize.

2d OFFICER.

The obfervation's juft---this way let's go;
Nor feen by him, intrude upon his thoughts---

    [*They go out on the oppofite fide, from that by*
     which Ceallachan *enters.*

         CEALLA-

CEALLACHAN *Solus.*

How ftrange is man!---his wifhes when obtain'd,
But fhow the fool he wants a fomething ftill---
Speed, fpeed, ye loitering moments of fufpence ;
No more diftract me with thy hopes and fears ;
Give me to know my fate, whate'er it be,
For dread of evil is the worft of ills.
But, lo ! my Duncan comes, and from his eye
The fparkling luftre fhoots forth heart-felt joy---
Enter DUNCAN.
Oh ! fpeak, my friend, and let thy words proclaim
What looks expreffive have already told.

DUNCAN.

Let joy unbounded reign throughout thy breaft ;
For know, my royal liege, the beauteous maid,
With modeft boldnefs owns a mutual flame---
" Go tell the generous prince you ferve," fhe faid,
" That every future blifs on him depends.
" Tell him, without a blufh, I own my love,
" And view with rapture the approaching hour
" That makes me ever his"---

CEALLACHAN.

---This, this is blifs ;
Thus to poffefs that moft fupreme delight,
The having pow'r to make my Stira blefs'd.
Now ev'ry gloomy view Defpair had bred,
But ferves to make the profpect pleafe the more.
O my friend, how can I e'er thy zeal repay
For tidings fuch as thefe !---

DUNCAN.

---I'm amply paid.
Wretched the man, whofe hard, unfeeling heart

Receives

Receives not pleasure from another's blifs :
But when my King, my friend, is happy made,
It then is ecstacy---

CEALLACHAN.

---I know it is,
To gen'rous souls like thine. These happy rites
Shall sheathe the deadly steel; our glitt'ring arms
No longer for destruction us'd, shall range
In pleasing order o'er our peaceful walls,
And give their splendor to the social feast.
Let other monarchs mad ambition boast,
Whilst I pursue love's happier scenes ;
Yield all my soul to its ecstatic bliss ;
Possess'd of Stira, court the peaceful shade,
Nor idly wander in pursuit of fame.

DUNCAN.

O flatter not thyself, my royal Lord ;
Necessity will oft oblige thee to resume
Thy arms neglected, and the martial field ;
Will oft oblige thee to forsake the couch,
Where love's delicious raptures lull thy soul ;
For tranquil scenes belong not to a throne.

CEALLACHAN.

Think not thy monarch's sword shall e'er be sheath'd,
When lawless insult calls its vengeance forth.
But still the moment of returning peace
Shall be embrac'd :---Still shall my tend'rest care
Be then employ'd to heal Destruction's wounds ;
Each peaceful art shall then renew its toil,
And Industry reflourish o'er the land.

DUNCAN.

DUNCAN.

Munfter, what happy days for thee's in ftore ;
Whofe monarch thus, in all his fchemes, purfues
His country's welfare and his people's good !

CEALLACHAN.

O rather fpeak the happinefs of him,
To whom the indulgent hand of Fate hath giv'n
A pow'r to gain fuch godlike ends as thefe.---
Is there a tranfport that this world can boaft,
Equal to that which in the bofom glows,
When from the low'ring brow of wretchednefs
You pluck its forrows, planting in their room
The chearful, glad'ning look, Content infpires ?
Oh ! grant not merit to the only act
That pays me for the troubles of a throne.

DUNCAN.

E'en Nature form'd thee for a king, and gave
A foul exalted as the rank you bear.

CEALLACHAN.

You view me, Duncan, with a partial eye,
But come, my friend, the beauteous Stira calls,
And all a lover's wifhes urge me hence.   [Exeunt.

SCENE changes to a different Part of the Wood.

Enter PHARON and a Danifh CAPTAIN.

PHARON.

Thou feeft where yonder hill its fummit rears,
Whofe fpacious fide's with branching oaks o'erfpread,
That hide in fhade the ftream that runs beneath---

Thither

Thither extend the left, in filent march,
And as the Irifh troop proceeds, advance :
Should you perceive the fignal we've agreed,
With rapid pace thy gallant foldiers lead
To join with mine, and intercept the foe.
Thou to the poft affign'd, and I to mine.   [*Exeunt.*

SCENE *changes again.*

CEALLACHAN, DUNCAN, *and the* IRISH
TROOPS *re-enter.*

DUNCAN.

Truft me my liege, fome treachery's on foot :
Amidft thofe diftant trees, the Danifh garb
This moment caught mine eye :---the clafh of arms
I alfo heard, or elfe mine ears deceive :
Allow me to explore the neighbouring wood,
And fee that fafety on thy fteps attend.

CEALLACHAN.

No dread of danger in my breaft I feel.---
But come, my Duncan, fatisfy thy doubts ;
Lead to the fpot from whence thefe fears arife.

SCENE *changes.*

Enter PHARON *and* Danifh CAPTAIN.

CAPTAIN.

This way they march, nor longer feek our walls :
A moment brings them up.---

PHARON.

PHARON.

      ---Then let us hafte
To ftop their purpos'd courfe; but ftrictly charge
Each valiant Dane to fpare the monarch's life ;---
For he who takes it, pays it with his own. [*Exeunt*.

SCENE *changes*.

Enter CEALLACHAN, DUNCAN, *and the*
IRISH *Train*.

CEALLACHAN.

Ha ! is every pafs befet ?---

DUNCAN.

      ---Each pafs is clos'd
With thronging Danes---one only choice remains,
To yield fubmiffion, or to part with life.---

CEALLACHAN.

Oh ! for a thoufand of my Dalgais now !---
But fay, my gen'rous friends, how beats each heart ?
Doth glory nerve each valiant warriors' arm ?
Will ye ignobly live, or bravely die ?

ALL.

We fcorn ignoble life---we'll bravely die.---

CEALLACHAN *draws his fword*.

Then, thus I hurl defiance at the foe.
What are ten thoufand flaves oppos'd to men
Who fight for freedom, and for glory burn !
Let's on, my gallant youths, there is the path
     E   That

That leads to Munfter, to each focial tie :
Think what your country, what your fires demand ;
Think of a monarch's wrongs, and follow me. [*Exeunt.*

[*Fighting is heard for fome time behind the Scenes, after which* Ceallachan *and* Duncan *enter engaged
with* Pharon, *and a number of the* Danes.]

PHARON.

Yield up thy fword, nor urge deftruction on.----

CEALLACHAN.

Yes, flave, when life's no more.----

PHARON.

         ----What madnefs this !
To force like ours, what is thy ftrength oppos'd?----
Submit, and tafte our mercy.----

CEALLACHAN.

         ----Thy mercy, wretch !
Thus I revenge a monarch's wrongs----

DUNCAN.

         ----And thus----
[*Whilft they are rufhing on the enemy, a party
comes behind and difarms them.*]

CEALLACHAN.

Off ! cowards off !----

DUNCAN.

----Unhand me, villains !----

PHARON.

PHARON.

Soldiers, your pris'ners guard with due refpect;
Our fcatter'd troops my care demands---

[*Exit.*

[*The* Danifh *Soldiers remain at a little diftance.*]

[Ceallachan *and* Duncan *come forward.*]

CEALLACHAN.

Oh, Duncan! I am fick at heart---behold
Thofe ftreams of blood, that lately flow'd for me---
Each valiant youth, who round me fought, hath paid
The tribute of his life, fave only you ;
Thou too art doom'd to meet a monfter's rage,
And to his vengeance bleed---All-gracious Heav'n
Heap forrows yet unheard-of on this head ;
But, oh ! in pity ceafe thefe cruel fhafts
That pierce me thro' the bofoms of my friends.

DUNCAN.

Let not one thought for me difturb thy mind ;
My friendfhip grew not by the foft'ring gales
That profperous fortune blows ; nor can the blafts
Of wint'ry ftorms, rais'd by adverfity,
Deftroy the hardy plant.---To die with thee ?
'Tis nought---have we not ftill fince earlieft youth,
Gone hand in hand ;---no feparate pleafures known ;
In joy, in grief, ftill equally partook ?
And would'ft thou then at laft fhake off thy friend ?

CEALLACHAN.

Let me embrace the nobleft of mankind.
Thus with the man whofe fad appearance fhows
A fhatter'd fortune and a clouded day ;
Whofe gay companions of his brighter hours,

E 2   Vanifh

Vaniſh with them, and leave him to his fate ;
If then a real friend appear, it chears
His drooping ſoul, his value well he knows,
And claſps the kind conſoler to his breaſt.

PHARON *enters, and ſpeaks.*

PHARON.

Moſt valiant King, and you brave Sir, muſt ſtraight
To Dublin's walls proceed---Sitrick commands,
And his commands I muſt obey---

CEALLACHAN.

---I know
Thou art his ſlave, nor ſhall I talk to thee
Of broken faith, and nations' rights betray'd---
Lead on, we'll follow, Sir---O now, my friend,
Undaunted let us meet this final ſhock,
The laſt that mortals know---Tho' none have pow'r
To ſhove misfortune back, or change the courſe
By Heav'n's high will decreed ; yet all may riſe
Superior to thoſe ills they can't prevent.
Hence, to that world we'll take our anxious flight,
Where ſacred Virtue only meets reward.

[*Exeunt.*

End *of the* SECOND ACT.

ACT III.

SCENE, *Palace.*

SITRICK *discovered in a Room of State,* a Captain
in waiting.

SITRICK.

GO tell the gallant Pharon, that Sitrick burns
To thank his faithful zeal.---Bid him conduct
His pris'ners here.---   [*Exit* Capt.
        ---My plan muft now fucceed---
This bar remov'd, my arms fhall quick prevail
O'er all Hibernia's Chiefs :---her fertile plains
Shall own me for their lord, and all her wealth
Shall foon be mine.---But then the world condemns,
Detefts the deed ; and brands my hated name
With ev'ry term that infamy can give.
Now confcience too uplifts her awful head,
And in the midft of all my triumphs
Stings my bofom with remorfe ;---deftroys each joy,
And every fcene difturbs---'   (*a long paufe.*)
        ---What---yield him up ?
Refign, forego the advantage I have gain'd ?---
Ambition and revenge forbid retreat,
And I obey.---Welcome, my faithful Pharon,

[PHARON *enters with* CEALLACHAN
DUNCAN, Danes, &c.]

Well

Well haſt thou fill'd the poſt to thee conſign'd,
Whate'er it fits me to beſtow, demand :
Thou ſhalt not aſk in vain.....

PHARON.

.....Thus to receive
My royal chief's applauſe, is great reward :
Yet Pharon's wiſhes would prefer a ſuit,
He fears might give offence.—

SITRICK.

—Speak freely then ;
For on my ſoul, ſo much I prize thy worth,
I know not ought I would to thee refuſe.

PHARON.

Embolden'd by this kindneſs of my lord,
Some fitter ſeaſon Pharon will preſume
To be thy ſuitor.—

SITRICK.

—Well then, be it ſo.—
At length, Ceallachan, our arms prevail ;
No more art thou victorious o'er the Danes ;
But now the priſ'ner of their conquering ſwords.—
Thou know'ſt what vengeance on thy head impells ;
Yet hear our mercy—If now thou wilt conſent
To what our terms require, thy liberty,
And Stira's hand, may ſtill be thine.—

(Ceallachan *gives a look of anger and contempt.*)

—Ha ! what !
Doſt thou behold me with an eye of ſcorn?

Doſt

Doſt thou not know my power? doſt thou not know
That if I will, this moment is thy laſt!—

(Ceallachan *repeats his look, and ſtill remains ſilent.*)

Again! nor even deign to anſwer me?
By Heav'n I'll break thy ſpirit, and teach thee, Prince,
Preſumption's due.—

CEALLACHAN.

    —Say'ſt thou, preſumption's due?—
Tho' to hold converſe with a wretch like thee,
Is far beneath the man whoſe actions flow
From the pure fountain of an honeſt heart;
Yet will I ſtoop to ſtrike thee with diſmay.
Soon ſhall my valiant Dalgais, and the tribes
That ſpread along the Shannon's fertile banks,
With ſwords high brandiſh'd tear thee from thy walls:
Soon ſhall they give thee what thy deeds deſerve;
Soon make thee an example to mankind;
That fear henceforth the villain may deter,
Where virtue binds not, and where honour fails.—

SITRICK.

Haſte, ſlaves, and bear this haughty monarch hence:
Let ev'ry keeneſt torture be prepar'd
That art can teach—when his disjointed limbs,
And mangled fleſh in agony ſhall writhe;
We'll ſee if thus he'll brave our wrath.—

CEALLACHAN.

    —Then learn
Inhuman Dane, ſuch cruelty is vain:
Perhaps this feeble fleſh may fail its lord;

       May

May tremble on the rack, and own its pangs:
But the pure foul fhall glory in its truth ;
Shall rife exulting to its kindred fkies,
And look with horror on a ftate like thine.

SITRICK.

Hence—lead him to his fate—

PHARON.

—Let me intreat
A fhort delay—when rage to reafon yields,
He'll quick comply.—

SITRICK.

—Well then, at thy requeft
He fees to-morrow's dawn.----But know, proud king,
If at the rifing fun you fhould refufe,
That Waterford and Cafhell's lofty tow'rs,
That Corke and Limerick's ample walls, with all
The towns of ftrength in Munfter's wide domain,
Be inftant yielded to the Danifh fway ;
Thy life fhall glut my vengeance !—

CEALLACHAN.

—Such threats are idle,
When apply'd to me—for know, I fcorn a life
That's in thy pow'r to give or take away.—

SITRICK.

When all the dread array of Fate appears,
Then wilt thou beg, perhaps, may beg in vain,
Nor gain the boon you afk !—

CEAL.

CEALLACHAN.

—Think'ft thou my foul
So little knows the firmnefs of a man,
That poorly frighted by the trick of woe,
Shock'd by a mere parade, I could refign,
A loyal nation to tyrannic fway?
Had you e'er felt the flame of patriot fire,
Whofe purifying blaze ennobles man,
And banifhes each bafe, each felfifh thought,
Far from the breaft wherein it deigns to dwell,
You then would know a monarch's fix'd refolve;
Would know, I court the terrors you difplay,
And, for my country's welfare, long to die!

SITRICK.

'Tis greatly talk'd---but know, this fingle day
Is thine. Confider well, and think on life.

CEALLACHAN.

And think on life!---Each word degrades thee more,
And pity almoft mingles with my rage.
But why thus talk to thee? where we defpife,
Silence is the beft reply.

SITRICK.

Wilt thou ftill dare
To brave our wrath? We'll try thefe boafting words.
Hafte, my Pharon, with chains this hero bind;
Let coarfeft food his hunger ferve, nor let
One ray of light illume his difmal cell.
In other walls let Duncan be confin'd.
Not e'en thy friend fhall fhare or footh thy woes;
Thou fhalt be prov'd.

F   CEAL-

CEALLACHAN.

   ---Come, and behold the proof---
Come, and behold me in the dungeon's gloom,
Superior to the ills that throng around;
And learn to value what thou can'ft not know.
Then quickly lead me to the ftroke of Fate;
With love of country throbbing at my heart
I'll meet the deftin'd blow, and fhow thee, Sitrick,
My life was in thy pow'r, but not my honour.

  [*Exeunt* Ceallachan, Duncan, Pharon, *Guards, &c.*

Manet SITRICK.

By Heav'n, to hear the vauntings of this man,
One would fuppofe he was the victor!

STIRA *enters in great diforder, and kneels.*

STIRA.

Oh, with a brother's eye behold me kneel,
Nor let a fifter's heart, with woe o'ercharg'd,
Burft from its feeble bounds, and rufh to death.
If e'er our parents to thy mem'ry rife,
Who with their laft, their lateft breath bequeath'd
My helplefs youth to Sitrick's care ! if e'er
You felt one fpark of fond paternal love
Arifing in thy breaft ; oh! grant my pray'r---
Let Munfter's King to freedom be reftor'd,
And blefs thy fifter with the man fhe loves.

SITRICK.

Away, thou ftain to Sitrick and thy race !
How dar'ft thou call our royal parents' fhades

         To

To witnefs to thy fhame?—degen'rate wretch
To let thy country's foe engage thy heart,
And warm thy breaft to love!——I'll caft thee off,
Nor own thee of my blood——

STIRA.

——Oh! think, my Lord,
And let thefe tears, this bleeding heart prevail.
'Twas you that rais'd my fond, expecting hopes,
To that delightful ftate where late they foar'd.
O do not then thus blaft each promis'd blifs,
Thus drive me to defpair!---

SITRICK.

---Thou wanton, ceafe---
Doft thou not blufh to own thy country's hate,
The object of thy bafe impetuous flame——
The man, of whom our babes with horror fpeak,
And weeping matrons curfe?——

STIRA.

——Wrong me not thus,
Nor wound a wretched fifter's fpotlefs fame.
No wanton paffion in my bofom dwells,
No thought that veftals might not wifh to own.
If 'tis a crime to fee and to admire,
Where ev'ry gen'rous tender virtue joins
To form the man——I gladly boaft my guilt.

SITRICK.

If thus thy tongue wilt riot in the praife
Of Sitrick's foe, farewell. I'll hear no more——

[STIRA

[STIRA *holds him.*]

STIRA.

Yet hear me, Sitrick, grant what I implore,
I will not afk thee for thefe promis'd rites ;
Such wifhes I'll refign—All I requeft
Is this——Reftore him to his country's arms ;
Let him be free, and may you be moft blefs'd.
Not e'en my forrows fhall difturb thy peace :
The mourning Stira, from the world retir'd,
Shall ne'er intrude one figh t' offend thine ear.
Beneath fome fhade my tears fhall harmlefs flow,
And o'er my cheeks in filence glide away,
Till in the grave thy fifter's griefs are laid,
And all is hufh'd within the peaceful tomb.

SITRICK.

Why wilt thou plead, to fave a life he fcorns?
The haughty monarch braves approaching fate :
My offer'd terms are treated with contempt!
E'en Stira's charms have loft their wonted force,
Nor can they now fubdue fo cool a lover.—

STIRA.

Alas ! had he, my Lord, but coolly lov'd,
He had not been by thee betray'd.——

SITRICK.

——In vain
You feek to change thy brother's fix'd refolve :
My terms accepted, can alone reftore
Ceallachan to liberty and thee.
Hafte then, employ perfuafion's utmoft art ;

With

With all that matchlefs beauty urge thy fuit,
Avert his ruin, and regain repofe.——

[*Exit.*

Enter BEDA, *as* SITRICK *goes out.*

BEDA.

O fay, my Stira, have thy tears prevail'd?
Have thy entreaties touch'd thy brother's foul?
O fay! is Munfter's monarch doom'd to die,
Or doth foft pity melt the tyrant's breaft,
And ward deftruction off?——

STIRA.

——Alas! my friend,
Still doubtful is his fate—if he confents
To Sitrick's terms, the hero yet is mine—
But, oh! thofe terms have been already tried,
Have been already treated with difdain.

BEDA.

O could you gain admittance to the King,
Perhaps all-powerful love might lend its aid,
Might change the firmnefs he fo lately fhow'd,
And raife up wifhes for a longer life.——

STIRA.

'Tis now my only hope—by Sitrick's will,
Thy Stira haftes to try this laft refource.
Oh! I will quickly feek the fuffering chief;
Ufe all the tender foftnefs of my fex,
Plead the fweet raptures that await on love,
Melt into tears, and fteal upon his heart:

Then,

Then, when I find him bending to my wishes,
Seize the fond moment, and obtain compliance. [*Exit.*

Manet BEDA.

Go, lovely maid, may angels wait your steps,
Inspire your tongue, and crown you with success.
No more I'll seek your nuptials to prevent,
No more to misery add the weight of guilt,
Nor be a rival, where I seem a friend.
How dreadful is a state of dark disguise,
When every word must studied be, before
It ventures forth—when every look is train'd,
And taught the guilty language of a lie?
Can the deceitful bosom ever know
A bliss like that which swells the noble heart,
Where conscious rectitude inspires each thought,
And proudly owns the dictates of the soul ?   [*Exit.*

SCENE *changes.*

Enter PHARON *and* CLEONES.

PHARON.

I seiz'd the fav'ring moment fortune gave,
And to the haughty Dane reveal'd my passion.
Beyond my hopes he list'ned to my suit,
Bade me expect his lovely sister's hand,
If at the rising of to-morrow's sun,
The monarch still reject his offer'd terms—

CLEONES.

My Lord, I would not willingly offend ;
Permit me, therefore, to with-hold my thoughts.

I've

I've learn'd indeed for to reſtrain my tongue,
But cannot utter what I do not feel.—

PHARON.

Nay, then you ſtill remember my offence,
Nor haſt thou yet forgiv'n my fooliſh raſhneſs.—

CLEONES.

Believe me 'tis long ſince forgot.—But ſay,
Why ſhould I wound the feelings of a friend,
And give a cenſure where he hopes applauſe?

PHARON.

O ſpeak, my friend, as thou wert wont to do,
When in our boyiſh days we firſt eſteem'd ;
When, from the joyous train of ſportive youths
We choſe each other out ; together roam'd,
Together chac'd our rural hours away.
Think of that friendſhip we ſo oft have vow'd,
Nor longer fear you can again offend.—

CLEONES.

Far different were thoſe days which you recall;
Then the pure ſoul, untainted by mankind,
In native innocence ador'd its God,
Diſplay'd the rich perfection Nature gave,
In love with virtue, and of vice afraid.
Oh! Pharon, what a foe to man is man?
When, from the peaceful ſhade of rural life,
They crowd together, corruption flows apace ;
Unheard-of crimes ariſe to curſe the world,
And puniſh men, for violated laws.

PHA-

PHARON.

Happy indeed, our youthful moments pafs'd;
Yet fituation cannot change the foul:
Are we not ftill the fame fond friends, Cleones?
Or art thou alter'd, and to Pharon falfe?

CLEONES.

I am the fame, but thou art chang'd indeed!
Before thy mad ambition led thee on
To feek for glory in the Danifh court,
How would'ft thou Pharon, have beheld thofe deeds,
Which now thy ready hand can ftoop to aid?
How would'ft thou then have view'd a king betray'd?
One too, whom e'en the malice of a foe
Might feek to cenfure, and yet feek in vain.
Oh! in thofe hours of unpolluted life,
Methinks I now behold thy glorious rage;
Thy ready fteel almoft unfheath itfelf,
And as the treacherous tale was told, thy eyes
Flafh lightning from their orbs, whilft ev'ry nerve
Grew big with manly indignation!—

PHARON.

—Alas,
I feel the juft reproach:—Yet fure, my friend,
When for the public, ftratagem is us'd:
When policy requires a hidden act,
The very colour of the deed is chang'd;
And that, which in the private fphere of life
Abhorrence claims---then merits our applaufe.

CLEONES.

Oh, Heav'n! where will mankind's prefumption end?
When thus they dare to alter thy decrees,

To

To change thofe laws their great Creator fram'd,
And give to villainy the praife of virtue !
If the affaffin, for the price of blood,
Stab in the dark, and give the hired blow ;
If from revenge the poniard be unfheath'd,
And buried in the heart for which 'tis drawn ;
You call it murder ; and as fuch you punifh:
But when the ftatefman acts beneath the mafk
Of feeming peace, and of fictitious treaty,
Till he with fafety can deftroy a foe ;
Both wealth and honours crown the very act
For which a lefs exalted villain bleeds !

PHARON.

Chide on, chide on ; for I have yet fo much
Of virtue left, as to admire Cleones.
O prove thyfelf a kind, a gen'rous friend ;
Point out the way by which I can regain
Thy loft efteem, and what is yet ftill more,
My own applaufe !—

CLEONES.

—O Pharon ! afk thyfelf;
For confcience is not dead within thy breaft :
Afk if Ceallachan deferves to die ;
Afk if the mourning Stira fhould be thine ;
Examine then the part which you have play'd,
And know the conduct you fhould now purfue.

PHARON.

Oh ! I will hafte, and try my utmoft fkill,
To fave the monarch's life, and fet him free ;

G   But

But to refign the fond, the flatt'ring hope,
Of Stira's being mine, is furely more
Than even Virtue can demand.——

CLEONES.

　　　　　　　　——You dream!
Where is the hope I aſk you to refign?
Doth not the lovely maid e'en now deplore
A captive lover and averted rites?
O haſte, my lord, a gen'rous paſſion ſhow,
With inborn greatneſs plead thy rival's claim:
Lead him to happineſs which can't be thine;
Wipe from her eye the pearly drop of grief,
And prove at leaſt that you deferve her love.——

PHARON.

　　Yes, then! my better angel, I will go;
Will drive this miſt of paſſion far away;
No longer plunge impetuous into guilt,
But be again the partner of thy virtues.

　　　　　　　　　　　　　　[Exit.

Manet CLEONES.

　　May Heav'n ſupport thee in the great refolve.
But, oh! I fear, like to the meteor's blaze,
'Twill for a moment ſhine, and then expire.
When firſt, untutor'd in the wiles of men,
In ſweet ſimplicity, I knew thee, Pharon,
Ne'er was a mind more richly grac'd than thine!
How could example then thus change thy ſeul?
But what cannot example do? at firſt
The ingenuous mind with horror views

　　　　　　　　　　　　　　The

The frightful form of vice.—But foon, alas!
The dire contagion fpreads.—We dare to do
What we but lately fhudder'd to behold.
Each finer feeling is by cuftom drown'd ;
We catch the reigning manners of the age,
And lofe abhorrence for the worft of crimes.

[*Exit.*

End of the THIRD ACT.

G 2

ACT IV.

CEALLACHAN *difcover'd in Prifon,*
with a fingle Taper burning.

[Comes forward.]

CEALLACHAN.

WHERE now the regal pomp and proud parade?
      Where now my thronging chiefs, eager to fhow
A real or fictitious zeal? and, oh! where now
The nuptial torch, and Hymen's blifsful rites?
The radiant fun ne'er fhed his golden beams
Around a happier monarch's brow, when laft
His bright effulgence blefs'd the world:
But thus the fabric moulders into duft,
Whofe bafe is founded on the ground of life.
Ah! foolifh man, who to the future blind,
By Fancy's gay creation fondly paints
Sweet fcenes of blifs that never can arrive:
Each paffing day the lov'd delufion proves;
Yet ev'ry day brings forth fome new deception.

[Turns, and fees STIRA *at the bottom of the Stage.]*

Ha! doth fome bright phantom mock a wretch?
Or can it be?—It is, it muft be fhe:
For fhe alone's poffefs'd of fuch a form!—

[Runs to her.

Oh! thou bright maid, who thus benignly fhines,

Amidft

Amidft furrounding gloom; Oh ! quickly fay,
Doth that foft bofom beat indeed for me ?
Do thofe fad tears from mutual paffion flow,
And is the bloody Sitrick only falfe ?

STIRA.

O think not hardly of thy Stira's faith !
No bafe deceit this bofom e'er hath known ;
By Sitrick's art I too have been deceiv'd,
No brighter profpect e'er a maid beguil'd :
To plunge her from tranfporting look'd-for blifs,
To all the matchlefs horrors of defpair.

CEALLACHAN.

Oh ! thou art truth itfelf,—in every look
I read the rich perfection of thy foul.
Oh ! let me wipe thofe courfing tears away ;
Let me infold thee in thefe longing arms,
Gaze on thy beauty, prefs thofe balmy lips,
Till loft in raptures of ecftatic blifs,
I tafte of heav'nly joys before I die.

STIRA.

Yet live, my lord, to love and me—if no more
Of pow'r depriv'd, to Munfter you'd return,
With thee to fome lone rural fpot I'll fly,
Sequefter'd from the world, with thee be blefs'd,
Nor think of royalty refign'd.—

CEALLACHAN.

—Oh ! no :
Tho' my foul pants for fuch a ftate with thee,
A thoufand reafons do my blifs obftruct,
And place eternal obftacles between.

STIRA.

STIRA.

What, tho' glory may not on the deed attend ;
Yet love its balmieſt influence ſhall ſhed,
Shall make us happieſt of the human race.
No pomp I ſeek, no glittering badge of power,
No ſplendid roof, no high repaſt demand ;
So thou art mine, I care not for ſuch toys.
With thee the humbleſt cot will ſtill delight ;
The ſimpleſt food, the coarſeſt dreſs will pleaſe :
With thee the pleaſing partner of each toil,
Theſe hands ſhall gladly labour, from the morn
Till in the weſt the evening ſun deſcends ;
Then by thy friendly arm upheld, I'll ſeek
The peaceful ſhelter of our ſweet retreat ;
There welcome in the night with vows of love,
And bury ev'ry care within thy arms.

CEALLACHAN.

Ah ! ceaſe ; ſuch unexampled love refrain :
Already doth my reſolution ſhake ;
To liſten longer would my fall complete.
Had Fortune plac'd me in an humbler ſphere,
How eagerly I'd ſeek ſome rural ſpot,
Far from the noiſe and buſtle of the world,
By woods emburied, and by rocks begirt :
There would I taſte true happineſs with thee ;
With thee, each ecſtacy of love enjoy ;
And bleſs the lowly lot whoſe peaceful toil
Ne'er led me from my Stira's charms away !
But now, my honour and my fame's at ſtake ;
Nay more, my love ; for love like thine muſt ceaſe,
When it no longer can eſteem.—

STIRA.

STIRA.

—Ah, talk not thus—
What is this honour, or this bubble fame,
Whofe airy praife, thus tempts us to forego
All real, for imaginary blifs ?—

CEALLACHAN.

What elfe but thefe could keep mankind in awe ?
Virtue and vice in one dark chaos hurl'd,
No bright reward would fpur the hero on;
No infamy the villain would deter.
But fay, doth Stira wifh me to comply ?
Would fhe embrace the king, whofe felfifh foul
Could meanly practice on a people's love ?
Could thus affaffinate the public weal !

STIRA.

'Gainft thee and virtue, I no longer plead.
O never, never quit thy glorious courfe !
—To yield our darling private paffions up,
When public good the facrifice requires ;
Is this world's bounds t' o'erleap—afpires to heav'n,
And treads upon the footfteps of a God.—

CEALLACHAN.

Thou heav'nly maid, for ever could I hear
Thofe accents fweet, which flowing from thy tongue,
Appear to be divine. Would but the fair
Thus plead in Honour's caufe ; would beauty thus
Our kind inftructor prove ; degraded vice
Would hang abafh'd, and feek its native gloom :
Benevolence, with pure unfpotted love,
Would then difpenfe their heav'nly joys around,
And with angelic blifs infpire mankind.

Enter

Enter Captain *to* STIRA.

CAPTAIN.

Madam, the royal Sitrick quick demands
Thy prefence.—

STIRA.

—Go, fay I fhall attend his will.
[*Exit* Capt.

And fhall we never, never meet again !
Is all my promis'd blifs for ever fled !
Is this to be the laft fad fcene of love !

CEALLACHAN.

O ftop thofe tears, they pierce me to the foul!
Terrors unknown now rife within my breaft,
Shake my refolves, and make a coward of me !
To part with life I nothing deem'd : but, oh !
To part with thee is more than I can bear !

STIRA.

Methinks I now behold thy mangled corfe—
Thy body writhing in the pangs of death !—
O fave me, fave me from the direful image !
The dread idea fires my heated brain,
And madnefs will enfue!—
[*She throws herfelf on his bofom.*

CEALLACHAN.

—Oh ! my lov'd Stira,
Yield not to fuch thoughts !---the pitying Heav'ns,
Who now behold our innocence and woes,
May yet, by fome unlook'd-for means avert
Impending ruin, and our blifs reftore.

STIRA.

STIRA.

Vain is the hope---no pitying Heav'ns avert
Thy haplefs fate : too furely wilt thou bleed ;
And, oh! diftracting thought, wilt bleed for me!

Enter CAPTAIN *again.*

CAPTAIN.

Thy royal brother fends once more, to bid
Thy inftant prefence.---

STIRA.

---Retire, I'll follow thee.

[*Exit* Capt.

CEALLACHAN, *embraces her.*

And muft we part? muft I refign thee then?
Oh! Stira, for ever could I hold thee thus;
Here clafp thee, till the hand of drooping age
No more obey'd the dictates of the foul :
E'en then, my clofing eyes fhould look on thee,
My fault'ring tongue pronounce thy darling name,
And the laft finking pulfe fhould beat with love.

STIRA.

O let me go, whilft yet 'tis in my pow'r!
My lips deny an utt'rance to my thoughts.
Oh! let thefe tears fupply the place of words,
And bid to thee, my lord, a fad farewell.—

[*Goes flowly out.—*Ceallachan *gazes after her—then
fpeaks.*]

CEALLACHAN, *Solus.*

Thus doth the wretch whom fome o'erwhelming wave
Hath fwept from off the deck, behold the fhip

H   Pafs

Pafs rapid thro' the deep—ftill as fhe goes,
His hopes of life decline ; no longer feen,
Defpair o'erpow'rs his foul ; he ftrives no more,
But yields, without a ftruggle, to his fate.   [*Exit.*

SCENE *changes to the Palace.*

Enter SITRICK *and* PHARON.

SITRICK.

What then, doth Pharon plead in fuch a caufe ?
Seeks he to loofe a lion from the toils,
Inflam'd by infult, and with vengeance fir'd ?
No, by the manes of my royal fire,
He yields fubmiffion to the Danifh arms,
Becomes a tributary vaffal to our fway,
Or falls a victim to his ftubborn honour.

PHARON.

O think, my lord, whilft yet to think is thine ;
Nor let ill-grounded fears miflead thy foul.
Gen'rous and noble is the captive king,
Above the paffions of a vulgar mind :
Give but thy lovely fifter to his arms,
Let liberty unpinion'd wait his fteps,
Not clogg'd with bafe conceffions ; and truft me, Sitrick,
You'll gain a friend, where you fufpect a foe.

SITRICK.

Ha ! do I wake ? is Stira held fo cheap,
That Pharon flights what he fo late implor'd?
Doth Sitrick ftoop to join his blood to thine,

That

That thou ſhould'ſt ſcorn the bounteous gift; ſhould'ſt
  praiſe
With laviſh tongue the man I hate, and prove
Ungrateful to the hand that rais'd thee?

PHARON.

     ——My Lord,
Is this ungrateful, when thus thy Pharon pleads
'Gainſt all his fondeſt wiſhes could demand?
When thus for Sitrick's welfare he'd reſign
Far more than life—the woman he adores?
O do not wrong thy ſervant's faithful zeal,
Nor wound a boſom that would bleed for thee!

SITRICK.

Forgive th' impetuous temper of thy Lord,
And know that he no longer doubts thy truth.
—But, lo! the mourning Stira hither comes,
And in the ſettl'd ſadneſs of her brow,
I read the haughty monarch's ſtern reſolve.

STIRA enters.

What then! hath female ſoftneſs urg'd in vain
Its fond attachment and the joys of love?
Could he unmov'd behold thoſe ſtreaming eyes,
Nor by compliance chace thy tears away?
Now by the immortal gods! if yet one drop
Of Denmark's royal blood courſe thro' thy veins,
And tell thee of thy birth, thou'lt be reveng'd!
Wilt to a fonder lover give thy hand,
E'en in the preſence of this haughty king;
And greatly ſhow, you've learn't to ſcorn the man
Whoſe pride's ſuperior to his love for thee!

STIRA.

Could he to felfish pleafures yield up all
That fpeaks the monarch, and adorns the man,
He would indeed deferve my fcorn. For know,
Tho' Stira feels each weaknefs of her fex;
Tho' unavailing woe muft caft a fhade
O'er every future hour; and grief unceafing,
Thro' a fad exiflence, wait me to the grave;
By all the powers of Heav'n I fwear,
I'd rather bear it all, than give my hand
Where forfeit honour was the price that gain'd it!

SITRICK.

No more fhalt thou abufe thy brother's patience
With idle nonfenfe and romantic folly.
Entreaties from this moment ceafe; and now
In me thou feeft a mafter, whofe pow'r fupreme
Muft be confefs'd——Madam, behold the man
Whom Sitrick deftines for thy lord——and learn
That my commands henceforth fhall be obey'd.

PHARON.

I'm loft again, and virtue is no more.

[*Afide.*

STIRA.

Doth Sitrick know fo little of my foul,
That thus he deals forth threats to fhake my truth?
Think'ft thou the maid Ceallachan prefers,
Can ever ftoop to own another Lord?
No! By that royal blood which fills my veins,
Which lifts my fex fuperior to its fears,
If death alone can fave my plighted faith,
In death I'll fhow thee what it is to love!

Enter

Enter a DANISH CAPTAIN *to* SITRICK.

CAPTAIN.

My Lord, my Lord, the Irish chief is gone !
By wond'rous means he———

SITRICK.

———Ha ! Ceallachan escap'd !———
Bring forth the treacherous guard———

CAPTAIN.

———My royal Lord,
Duncan alone hath from thy troops escap'd :
His garb forsaken, and a bar remov'd
Declare the wondrous means by which the chief
Obtain'd a passage to the waves below.
Th' astonish'd Danes e'en yet their senses doubt,
So daring was the act ; and all agree
He perish'd e'er he reach'd the foaming deep,
Or in the raging billows met his fate.

SITRICK.

'Tis well : I'm calm again. Double the guard
That watches o'er the eastern tow'r, and see
That future vigilance for this atone.

[*Exit* Captain.

Nay then, since bars, since waves oppose in vain,
My tardy vengeance shall no longer sleep.
Madam, prepare my pleasure to fulfil :
For know, e'er yet the moon's reflected light
Doth for the wearied sun illume the heav'ns,
The holy priest shalt give thee to my friend,

Whilst

Whilft Munfter's King beholds the facred rites,
And learns to dread that power he now contemns.
Nay, fpare thy tears; they on a lover fail'd;
And truft me, Stira, will not now avail.

[*Exit* Sitrick.

PHARON.

Permit me, beauteous maid, to foothe thy woes,
And fhare at leaft the grief I cannot cure.
If to adore thee more than all thy fex;
If to have lov'd in filence from that hour,
When firft thofe heav'nly beauties caught mine eye,
Can merit a return, 'tis Pharon's right.
O let me then thus feize thy hand——Thus fpeak---

STIRA.

Away...thou bafe infulter go,---nor prove,
That every virtue hath forfook thy breaft!
My forrows would be private, Sir——not feen
By fuch as thou art!——

PHARON.

——O kill not with thy fcorn,
The man who loves thee; to diftraction loves----
But give thy pity, if thou giv'ft no more.

STIRA.

O Heav'ns! doft thou prefume to talk of love?
Love is the produce of a generous foil,
Shoots forth luxuriant in the noble mind,
Is nurs'd by virtue, and by honour fed.
It fprings not in the tainted heart,
Nor dwells in fouls like thine.——

PHA-

PHARON.

——Oh! wrong me not.
Could'ft thou behold the feelings of this heart,
No longer would thefe keen reproaches flow.

STIRA.

Thy *virtues* are indeed to me unknown.
Unlefs the blood of innocence betray'd,
Unlefs fubfervience to a tyrant's will,
Be rank'd as fuch—but hear me e'er I go :
Not all the power of him thou calleft lord,
Shall ever force me to be thine---for know,
That death is welcome, when compar'd to thee.

[*Exit.*

Manet PHARON.

' Is death then welcome, when compar'd with me ?
No, no; when paffion ceafes, other thoughts
Will fill thy breaft, and life again be priz'd.
Tho' now the objeft of thy hate, the hand of time
Will change thy foul, and make me dear to thee.---
With kind attention, and unceafing love
I'll melt thy ftubborn heart---and make thee own
That Pharon merits——

CLEONES *enters.*

——Ha ! Cleones here !—
I dare not meet his eye. Let me withdraw,
Nor feem to have perceiv'd that he approach'd.

[*Exit.*

CLEONES *Solus.*

My Lord—Cleones would addrefs thine ear—
He fhuns me then, and thus declares his vow
Forgotten,

Forgotten, and his purpose chang'd—In vain
I've fought to call extinguish'd virtue forth;
In vain have fought to fave this godlike King.—
Oh, what a ftate is mine? my grateful foul
Bound to Ceallachan by ties moft ftrong,
Now fees the hour of fate draw near, without
A ray of hope.—Oh, thou Almighty Power,
Supreme of Heav'n! an humble fuppliant hear—
Grant me the means this hero to preferve;
Give me to pay the mighty debt I owe him,
And in his ftead let me to vengeance bleed.

[Exit.

End of the FOURTH ACT.

ACT V.

SCENE, *Palace of* Dublin.

STIRA, BEDA.

STIRA.

THE hour of fate draws near—the chiefs are met,
  The holy prieft prepares the folemn rites,
Waits but a nod th' Almighty to blafpheme,
And give a fanction to the worft of crimes.
O fay, then, Beda, is thy friend forgot?

BEDA.

O no, my Stira, I have been too true,
Nor broke a promife I fo rafhly made.
                              [*Shows a Phial.*
Behold the dreadful gift that friendfhip brings.

STIRA, *fnatches the Phial.*

Thus let me feize the precious draught, and blefs
The bouкteous hand from whence it came.

ATTENDANT *enters to* STIRA.

ATTENDANT.

Thy royal brother with impatience waits
Till you appear—for you alone delay
Th' expected rites, and univerfal joy.

                    I   STIRA.

STIRA.

Go tell thy mafter, Stira comes—and comes
Prepar'd for thefe expected rites.—Away—

[*Exit* Attendant.

Yes, Sitrick, this fhall free me from thy power;
This fhall preferve from violation's hand,
And fhow the wondering world how Stira lov'd.—

[*Drinks.*

'Tis done—No nuptial torch fhall now difplay,
The wretched victim of a brother's will.
But in its ftead, the funeral taper fhall
Diffufe its fickly beams around my corfe,
And add frefh horror to the difmal fcene.
O what a change is this ! But come, my friend,
We will obey the fummons of thy Lord—

[*Exeunt.*

S C E N E *changes to a Room of State,*
difcovering Sitrick, Pharon, Prieft, Danes,
&c. Cleones *thoughtful, and feparate*
from the reft.

S I T R I C K, *to an Attendant.*

Once more require the princefs to attend.
Go fay that Sitrick and that Pharon waits;
And fee that prompt compliance doth enfue.

[*Exit* Attendant.

[*To* CLEONES.]

And thou, Cleones, bring the captive king.
Firft fhall this haughty monarch own our fway,

Then

Then shall he—

       [A great noise is heard.

 —Ha! what strange alarm thus strikes our ear—
Thus rends the vaulted roof with martial sounds,
Of diftant war?—

Enter CAPTAIN.

CAPTAIN.

     ——To arms! to arms! my Lord,
Nor lose a moment—Already are our walls
Afcended by the foe—With dreadful fury
On they rush, and every tongue cries Vengeance---
Each his fellow urges on, and shouts
" Our King we'll free, his horrid wrongs revenge,
" Or perish all."——

SITRICK.

    —Ha! the troops of Munfter here!
This inftant shall their monarch die :—take this—

      [Gives a Signet to Cleones.

Bury thy poniard in his heart, and say,
'Twas Sitrick fent thee :—away!—

        [Exit Cleones

     — Now to the fight
We'll lead our valiant Danes; with fury meet,
And drive thefe rash invaders from our walls.

        [Exeunt.

    I 2 SCENE

SCENE *changes to the Prifon.*

CEALLACHAN *difcover'd fleeping on the Ground—*
CLEONES *enters and gazes on the* King.

CLEONES.

Happy the man whofe uncorrupted foul
No guilty deed difturbs :—calm and ferene,
Amidft impending ills, he lives in peace—
Stretch'd on the earth is blefs'd with gentle flumbers,
Which fplendid roofs, and beds of fofteft down
Oft court in vain.—But, lo ! the prince awakes.—

CEALLACHAN, *(rifing).*

Speak—what fecret purpofe brings thee to thefe walls?

CLEONES, *fhewing Signet and Poniard.*

See this, and this, brave prince, and guefs the reft.

CEALLACHAN.

I guefs it all, and am prepar'd to die.—
Thou feem'ft difturb'd; humanity calls forth
Thy pity for my fate, and ftops thy arm !—
Fear not to ftrike the blow—'tis Sitrick's act ;
And all the guilt belongs to him.—

CLEONES.

　　　　　　　—View me :
This face examine well—recollect'ft thou ought
That tells thee we have met before ?—

CEALLACHAN.

　　　　　　　—Thou art
To me unknown ;—nor can I recollect,
That e'er I faw thee till this hour.—
　　　　　　　　　　CLEONES.

CLEONES.

—Then, thus
I execute a tyrant's fell command.

[*Throws away the Dagger, and unbinds him.*

Haft thou forgot that day, when funk to earth
I begg'd for life, nor did in vain implore?—
Thy fword uplifted, ready to defcend,
Fell harmlefs to the ground;—Thy boon be thine,
Thou cried'ft; if e'er a foe beneath thy arm
Shall fink, fpare thou his life, and I'm repaid.—
Oft have I wifh'd fome blefs'd occafion fince,
This debt to pay, and thus 'tis now difcharg'd.
Thy troops now ftorm the fouthern fide;—take this.—

[*Gives* Ceallachan *a fword.*

Thefe walls no longer thee detain.—For me,
I'll hafte to where the thickeft fight prevails;
There in my country's caufe provoke my fate!
This act forbids me to furvive.—

[*Exit* Cleones.

Manet CEALLACHAN.

—He's gone!
O may fome guardian power his purpofe thwart,
And fave him from himfelf!—Is't poffible!
My troops already here!—How can it be!—
But now's no time for thought—This way leads forth.

[*Exit.*

SCENE

SCENE *changes to* SITRICK's *Palace.*

Enter DUNCAN, IRISH OFFICERS, Soldiers, &c.

DUNCAN.

No tidings of our monarch yet?—Thofe gates
Thrown wide, which late the King confin'd, declare
Some dreadful deed. O! fhould he be no more,
What joy can vict'ry yield, or conqueſt give?
Let's haſte and learn his fate, whate'er it be :—
But, hark! fome one with haſty ſtep draws near :—

CEALLACHAN *enters.*

'Tis he !—he lives !—and all my fears are o'er.—

CEALLACHAN.

Come to my arms, my lov'd, my gallant friend :
Words are too poor to fpeak thy prince's thanks,—
And ye my brave, my faithful warriors all
Accept th' o'erflowings of thy monarch's heart ;
Whofe grateful foul fhall well repay thy love,
But never can forget it.—

ALL.

        —For fuch a king,
Who would not fight? who would not die ?—

CEALLACHAN.

        —Once more
I thank ye all :—now Duncan let me know,
By what unlook'd-for means I fee thee here !—

                DUNCAN.

DUNCAN.

Then briefly thus :—Beneath night's friendly ſhade
I gain'd the waves that waſh'd my priſon's baſe,
And reach'd the ſhore without theſe hoſtile gates.
Not many hours had I purſu'd my way,
When to the right, amidſt the trees I ſpy'd
The glare of arms ;—the moon's full orb diſplay'd
The forms of men, and the quick ear beſpoke
Approaching ſteps :—alarm'd, I chang'd my courſe,
And to the left prepar'd to fly :—juſt then,
A party ruſhing forth oppos'd my way :
But, what my glad ſurprize ! when I beheld
Theſe dear companions of my earlieſt arms :
My father led them on : from him I learn'd,
Some few had ſcap'd unnotic'd from the fight,
Had reach'd his camp, and told the treach'rous deed :
Enrag'd he march'd th' impatient troops,
And thus unlook'd-for are we here.—

CEALLACHAN.

                              — But ſay,
How was the victory gain'd ?—I burn to know
The glorious fight ;—Haſte, let me hear it all.—

DUNCAN.

Fir'd by my tale, we quickly reach'd theſe walls,
And led our furious troops againſt the foe :
The Danes ſurpris'd, at firſt made no defence ;
We gain'd the wall, and beat their feeble guard :
But ſoon the day was chang'd ; their ſwarming troops
Clos'd up each gap of death, and ſeem'd t' increaſe,
Not leſſen by our ſlaught'ring ſwords :—in vain
Our little band oppos'd their dauntleſs breaſts,

                                        To

To all the shock of war : Their numerous foes
With unremitting fury drove them on,
To where a dreadful precipice o'erhangs
The briny wave ; despair fill'd ev'ry heart,
And certain death appear'd on ev'ry hand :
When, lo ! the valiant Fingal, ever first
Bright glory's path to tread, on Sitrick rush'd,
And grasp'd the tyrant in his dreadful arms !
Vengeance, he cry'd ! and with a furious spring,
From off the rock he leap'd ! another chief
Th' astonish'd Pharon seiz'd with equal rage,
And copied Fingal's god-like deed !—The Danes
A moment stood, and fearful gaz'd below.
Such desperate acts their fortitude subdu'd ;
Such desperate acts our troops inspir'd ;—They fled,
And conquest crown'd our arms.—

CEALLACHAN.

　　　　　　　　　　—O glorious men !
Such deaths as yours make even conquest dear.
But such men do not die !—their deeds immortal,
Borne on the wings of time, for ever live ;
For ever claim the tribute of applause !
Eternal honours wait their sacred shades,
And from their ashes future heroes spring !

DUNCAN.

My royal liege, among the captive Danes
One chief was ta'en, who seem'd to court his fate ;—
Ne'er did these eyes behold a braver warrior.—

CEALLACHAN.

Ha ! conduct him hither.

　　　　　　　　　　[*Exit* Duncan.
　　　　　　　　　　Mean

—Mean time, my friends,
Let no rude noife difturb this facred roof.
Far be the din of arms remov'd from hence ;
Nor let one hoftile deed proclaim us victors ;
For here my Stira dwells. I'll feek her ftraight,
And foothe her troubled fpirits into reft.

                              [*Exit.*

[CEALLACHAN *goes out on one fide, Soldiers
    on the other.*]

SCENE *opens, difcovering* STIRA *ftretch'd
    on a Couch, as if dead ; Attendants weeping
    round her.*

Enter CEALLACHAN.

What mean thefe founds of woe ?—Celeftial pow'rs !
Do I behold my Stira thus !—

                              [*Kneels by her.*
                    —Oh ! lovely maid,
Here will I gaze, here ftay while life remains !
O look on me as thou wert wont, and glance
That foft delicious fondnefs to my foul :
O let thofe balmy lips once more pour forth
Harmonious numbers to my ravifh'd ears.
Alas ! thofe eyes have loft their melting fweets ;
Thofe lips no more their heav'nly founds difpenfe ;—
Death revels over every charm !—
Hark !—fhe calls !—fhe chides my loitering hand !—
                    [*He ftarts up, and draws his fword.*
I come ! I come ! and thus—

            [BEDA *runs in, and feizes his Arm.*

        K   BEDA.

BEDA.

— This rashnefs ceafe ;
And learn from me, that Stira yet furvives :
By me deceiv'd, no poifon hath fhe ta'en,
But in its ftead a draught of wond'rous pow'r,
Which for a time each fenfe doth lull to reft,
As if th' infranchis'd foul had bid adieu
To its frail dwelling.—

CEALLACHAN.

—Do not trifle with defpair;
But as you hope for happinefs to come,
Tell me if this ftrange tale doth bear the ftamp
Of holy truth !—

BEDA, *pulls out a Phial.*

—This fhall anfwer all thy doubts:—
[Applies it to STIRA.
Behold ! the lily yields its fickly hue,
And the rich ftreams of life renew their courfe.—

CEALLACHAN.

She breathes !—her eye refumes its wonted luftre,
And the pale cheek regains its blooming honours.—
[Turns to BEDA.
Yes ! my guardian angel, fhe doth furvive !
Yet fhall my charmer live and make me blefs'd.

STIRA *raifes herfelf, and looks wildly round.*

Surrounding fpirits, fay ! what manfion this,
Where Stira's doom'd to dwell !—methinks thefe walls
Are not unknown !—My lov'd attendants too !
Sure that is Beda ! and, oh ! thou lov'd fhade,
[To Ceallachan.
Is

Is Heav'n indeed thus kind, to give me thee?—

CEALLACHAN.

My lovely fair, recall thy wand'ring fpirits;
Thou haft not yet thy debt to nature paid :
No deadly poifon tears my Stira hence ;
But years of blifs fhall crown thy virtues here!

BEDA.

Forgive a fraud by friendfhip prompted, and live
A happinefs to tafte, unknown to me.
I'll bid the world adieu ; and now devote
The remnant of my days to holy deeds.
Farewell.—Oppofe me not—nor vainly feek
To change the fettl'd purpofe of my foul.

[*Exit* Beda.

STIRA.

Since thus refolv'd, O may that peace be thine
Which holy deeds deferve !—And now my Lord,
O tell me, where is Sitrick?—Whatever crimes
His foul debafe, he is my brother.—

CEALLACHAN.

—Alas!

He lives no more.—

STIRA.

And by thy arm he fell?

CEALLACHAN.

O no ! my love ;—this hand could ne'er have fhed
Thy brother's blood :—Before I join'd my troops,
Th' unhappy Dane from Fingal met his fate.

K 2   Nay,

Nay, weep not thus; but fay, thou beauteous maid,
When may I hope—

STIRA.

   —Oh! talk not now of love!—
Already doft thou know, how dear thou art.
When Stira ought to give her hand—on you,
And you alone, fhe will beftow it.—

CEALLACHAN.

   —Enough.
Forgive a lover's ardour; and know, my fair,
Thefe nicer feelings do the more endear thee.—

DUNCAN *enters, with* CLEONES *in Chains.*

DUNCAN.

Behold, my liege, the Dane, whofe furious arm—

CEALLACHAN *runs to* CLEONES.

And do I fee my kind deliverer thus!—

     [*Turns to Soldiers.*
Unloofe thefe chains—to him ye owe your king!

     [*They take his chains off.*
Say, gen'rous Dane, what can a monarch give,
That worth like yours, wilt honour with acceptance?

CLEONES.

Moft noble king, one only boon I afk—
Let not the Danes to juft refentment fall:
Forget thofe wrongs, which but difgrac'd thy foes;
And having conquer'd them, thyfelf fubdue,

       CEAL.

CEALLACHAN.

Such worth as thine for all thofe wrongs atone.—
No power I claim o'er Denmark's fons, fave that
Of making thee their Lord.—

CLEONES.

    —With grateful thanks,
Permit me to decline this purpos'd rank;—
It fuits not with the man—

CEALLACHAN.

     —Urge not too far
This nicenefs of thy foul: none can demand
A fuller proof of moft exalted worth :
Thou'rt form'd to rule; nor will I be denied.
      [Turns to DUNCAN.
Go loofe the chains of ev'ry captive Dane ;
Banifh their fears, and tell them they are free :
Then fee, my Duncan, that our valiant troops
Elated with fuccefs, opprefs them not ;
Nor bafely give an infult to the fall'n.

(Addreffes the Audience.)

When in the field we meet oppofing foes ;
When fteel to fteel is clos'd in deadly ftrife,
Let Rage infpire, and Fury ftalk at large :
But when the fortune of the day is caft ;
When in the vanquifh'd we no longer meet
Contending arms—let Mercy walk abroad,
The conquer'd foothe, and mitigate their pain ;
The dying comfort, and the wounded heal.
Succefs indeed our admiration draws ;
But 'tis Humanity deferves applaufe.

        [Exeunt omnes.

EPILOGUE.

By the AUTHOR.

Spoken in the Character of STIRA.

NAY, *stop that rising grin—I come not here,*
  To raise a laugh, or wound the modest ear.
No wedding-jest ; nay, not one double phrase,
Shall make the timid blush, or wanton please.

  Tho' fix'd by custom, that some comic strain
Should soothe your woes, and mitigate your pain ;
Our bard presumes to wear a solemn face ;
To quit the beaten path of sly grimace ;
Gives the shrill notes of laughter to the wind,
And to reflection leaves the feeling mind.

  Ye Fair, attend ! like me still faithful prove,
Yet first, like me, with caution fix your love.
Let no soft nonsense steal upon the heart ;
Be not the captives of each coxcomb's art :
But when with honour manly sense unites,
And the fond lover all your love invites ;
With freedom own—nay, glory in the flame,
And think unshaken truth your noblest fame.

  Ye gen'rous Youths, this godlike hero view,
His virtues copy, to his worth prove true.
When war's dread clangor gives the loud alarm,
Let fury nerve each daring warrior's arm :

But,

But, in these hours of soft endearing peace,
Let horrid rage and civil discord cease:
No more unsheath the ornamental sword,
Nor combat for a rash unguarded word.

Somewhat there was the Poet bade me say,
To deprecate your wrath, and save his play.
Oh—'twas to tell you 'tis his first offence—
But be not trick'd by any such pretence;
For, tho' I dare not speak—'twixt you and I,
He ne'er again will at your mercy lie.

THE END.